Love is Like the Universe

Special Edition

includes *Flying on the Wings of the Angels of Love*

Love is Like the Universe

Special Edition

Anne Steinemann

Sky Parlor Publications™ · Nevada City, California

ISBN: 979-8-9866506-6-1 (paperback)
ISBN: 979-8-9866506-7-8 (e-book)

First edition published August 2023

This book consists of previously published and new material as follows:

-Previously published: *Love is Like the Universe* © 2021 by Anne Steinemann (ISBN: 9798774558469); copyright includes Anne Steinemann's Preface. Foreword © 2021 by John R. Barrie.

-Previously published: *Flying on the Wings of the Angels of Love* © 2022 by Anne Steinemann (ISBN: 978-0-578-29175-8); copyright includes Anne Steinemann's Preface. Foreword © 2022 by John R. Barrie. (Note: section headings have been added to this edition of *Flying on the Wings of the Angels of Love*.)

-Newly published: "About the Author" biography © 2023 by John R. Barrie.

-The photo of "Anne Steinemann" (wearing pearl necklace, from Sept. 2006) by the UW Media Office @ <https://commons.wikimedia.org/wiki/File:Anne_Steinemann_42.tif> is licensed under CC BY-SA 4.0 / Cropped and desaturated from original.

-The photo of "Anne C. Steinemann" (wearing Cross necklace, from June 2019) by Alistair Bone @ <https://commons.wikimedia.org/wiki/File:Anne_C._Steinemann.jpg> is licensed under CC BY-SA 4.0 / Cropped, brightened, and desaturated from original.

-The image "Love at Cross" from clker.com is in the public domain.

-Cover Photo © 2023 by John R. Barrie.

Cover and interior design by Sky Parlor Publications™
in consultation with Anne Steinemann.

Sky Parlor Publications™ is a registered trademark
in the United States of America.

Sky Parlor Publications™
P.O. Box 252
Nevada City, CA 95959
skyparlorpublications.com

Dedication

To all my loved ones,
to my father and mother,
and to my Lord Jesus.

–Anne Steinemann

Editor's Preface

For this Special Edition of *Love is Like the Universe*, Anne Steinemann's two books of spiritual sayings have been combined. A new biographical section is appended that recounts Anne's extraordinary life and her ongoing ministries.

Within these pages, readers will find a treasury of Anne's complete aphorisms from the original editions of *Love is Like the Universe* and *Flying on the Wings of the Angels of Love*. Each of her sublime sayings makes a profound impression precisely because of its brevity.

What is abundantly clear when one reads these sayings is just how powerfully they come alive in one's soul. Like a seed from Heaven, they are capable of taking root inside oneself and springing to life. As if divinely inspired, these maxims are charged with immense spiritual energy. They can help uplift and transform a person's outlook. One can thereby feel the peace of Jesus, the love of God, and the joy of Heaven in this very life.

We hope that readers will benefit from these inspirational sayings of Anne Steinemann, now collected in this Special Edition.

John R. Barrie

SPECIAL EDITION CONTENTS

Love is Like the Universe

by

Anne Steinemann

Table of Contents

Foreword

Among her many notable achievements during a distinguished career of accomplishments, Anne Steinemann, Ph.D., is recognized as the most highly cited scholar internationally in her research field. But Anne is also a devout lifelong Catholic who has striven with the same ardor to practice her spirituality in daily life. Significantly, these pithy sayings of hers stem from her personal experience, which imbues them with tremendous spiritual power. As Jesus authoritatively stated, "Whosoever hears these words of mine and puts them into practice is like a wise person who builds their house upon a rock" (Mt. 7:24).

This little book of Anne's inspirational sayings is infused with the living spirit of Jesus. The overarching theme is: love God, love all, love unconditionally, then love even more! Anne elegantly reminds us time and again that nothing else matters in life except to manifest this divine love at all times, under all circumstances. Within these beautifully expressed aphorisms, Anne echoes the profound, transformative words of Jesus: Love God and Love One Another. The reader is encouraged to open their heart and allow Anne's insights to settle into the deepest recesses of their soul. In this innermost part of one's being, a divine alchemy occurs whereby a receptive soul becomes filled with the limitless, all-encompassing divine love that Jesus taught. Because, in the end, in the thoughtful, luminous words of Anne Steinemann, "The only thing that lasts is love."

John R. Barrie

Preface

Ever since a little girl, I was consumed with big questions, such as, "What is the meaning of life? What should I be doing with my life?" My quest for answers led me to read everything I could read, talk with everyone I could talk with, from all faiths and no faith, to find out The Truth. I wanted a faith based on reason, not on a feel-good feeling or wishful thinking. This pursuit led me to a seemingly simple but universally pure answer: *Love*. Then *Love God and Love One Another*. And then *Jesus is The Way, The Truth, and The Life*. This truth has been my foundation, my compass, and my joy throughout my life.

Along this journey, I wrote down reflections or truisms that occurred to me, and I amassed quite a collection over thirty years. This little book is a selected compilation, in hopes they may help you on your journey. I thank John R. Barrie for his invaluable help in making this book and bringing it to light. I also thank, in special and heartfelt ways, John Eggers, Jimmy Kelley, Timothy Stephens, and Colleen Wainwright. Finally, I thank all the people whom I have known and loved, and who have loved me. This book is dedicated to them.

Anne Steinemann
Christmas 2021

Love

God is Love. Love is God. God is infinite, perfect, immortal love. Love as we know it on earth is God manifested. We are all lights of the world and we are here to spread God's love. We are vehicles of love, with infinite potential to love.

We are all equally children of God, but we all have different gifts. We all work together for the same goal: to become one with God, and with one another. We are here to bring ourselves to perfection (closer to God) through love, and to help others to perfection through our love of them and our manifestation of love in our lives.

Love is the goal; life is our classroom. We see, learn, and demonstrate how love can transform, help, and heal. We are here in life to learn about love.

The meaning of life is not to live – it is to love.

The soul wants to love, and the soul wants to be loved. The soul also wants unconditional, eternal, and infinite love. That love cannot go away. Something cannot become nothing. If the world blows up tomorrow, the thing that will remain is the love that we have generated.

We are here for love. We survive in order to love. Love is what lasts.

The primary goal is love, not survival. Survival is a wonderful side effect of love. But survival is not the ultimate meaning. Instead, the meaning of all is love.

It's all about love, and love is all about what you can do for other people and for the world.

Love means dying to self. You stop focusing on your own needs, your own survival, and start focusing on God and others.

Time and space are irrelevant to love. Although, while we are in this human and earthly dimension, time and space are used to demonstrate and experience love.

Love is an absolute truth. It would exist regardless of humans. We are instruments of love; we are here to create and spread love.

The ultimate test of love is to do the right thing, to do what is loving, even though the world may think it's crazy, and even though it goes against what would be best in terms of the physical body.

Love transforms. Love heals. Love produces miracles. The real miracles are not necessarily the physical miracles, but the miracles of the heart.

Love is a verb. It is not just some amorphous halcyon concept. Love in action is: gleeful self-sacrifice; knocking yourself out for the sake of another, and smiling inside the whole time; being generous from what you want yourself, not just from your excess; having one banana left to eat and giving it to someone else to make them happy.

If the human brain is fallible, then human knowledge can also be fallible. The only thing we truly know is love. The experience and transmission of love in any form, even if involving fallible humans, is valid and immortal.

Humans are imperfect, but their intention to love is perfect.

We are immortal. Love is life. Love is what never ends. The seeds of love we sow in this life blossom throughout eternity.

Love is like the universe: it's infinite and keeps expanding.

God

God loves us, infinitely and eternally. God made us. God loves us more than we can ever imagine. Think of what we'd do for someone we love, and God loves us even more. He only wants the best for us. The best is ultimately what will be loving. We want that outcome, too. So it's a great thing: our incentives are aligned.

Each person needs to search for the truth, to build a relationship with God. You must search to find God, and to open your heart to God.

Trust God. He knows the whole story, all the chapters. You just see some middle chapter headings. What you may think is unfair or horrible at the time will really turn out to be all for the best.

Focus on process, not just outcome. Do what you know to be loving, do the best you can do, and the outcome is up to God.

Here I am, with an awareness, and I had nothing to do with my creation or with the resources that keep me in this creation. All I know is that I have love in my heart, and I am called to love others and to glorify God however He wants me to.

You can't put your security in a job (or hard work, or health, or anything earthly). All of that can be taken away in an instant. You have to put your security in God.

To love Him, regardless of what life brings, and to just want to be with Him: That's unconditional love.

Jesus

Jesus provided us an instruction manual for our lives through the scriptures. He was very clear on what we should do and what we should not do with our lives.

Jesus focused on physical healing and on forgiveness of sins. But physical healing was not the main point – it was spiritual healing. (Besides, physical healing is just temporary.) It's the repentance – the conversion toward God – that's eternal. However, physical healing got people's attention. They realized that Jesus was who He said He was.

We are all parts of the body of Christ. It is like a human body: each cell is unique, each cell has the information of the entire body, and each cell depends on the other cells for the overall functioning. We are absolutely interconnected and interdependent.

Paradoxes, as Jesus taught: To gain your life you must lose your life (love is self-denial, a focus on others, putting others before yourself). To be wealthy in the kingdom of heaven you must forsake earthly wealth (don't put your security in material, transient things; the only thing that lasts is love).

Seek to radiate Christ in all situations: to be cheerful when in pain; to endure great pain for the sake of the greater good; and to be kind to those who may be unkind to you.

Good Friday turned into Easter Sunday. The suffering on the cross was one day. The Resurrection is eternal.

One Another

Make other people feel loved – let them know what a joy and blessing they are, how much you love to be with them, how it doesn't matter what they do or don't do or what physical or mental state they're in – that it's just such a complete joy and honor to be with them.

Be always kind. Never do anything (knowingly or willingly) unkind.

It's easy to be nice to people who are nice to you. It's a supreme testimony of love to be nice to people who aren't necessarily nice to you. A caveat: you can't keep walking back into the sword if people are harming you. Jesus wasn't a doormat. He walked away, but with love.

Everyone you meet, give them your full and enthusiastic attention, so they are the most important person in the world. Find something nice to say about them. Find some way to make them smile and make them feel special and beloved, because they are.

Affirm people whenever you can. Notice and express appreciation for what people do. Say, "Thank you for the beautiful job you do cleaning these facilities. I can only imagine what you have to see and deal with each day, and I really admire and appreciate all your work, and also that you are doing it all with a smile."

Write letters of commendation for service staff, such as fast-food workers and bus drivers. Be extra nice to people whom may not always hear nice things, such as call center staff and telephone solicitors – they are just trying to keep a job and raise a family.

Ask a homeless person what their favorite meal would be, and go get it for them. Even better, spend time to listen to them, to smile, to sit down with them, to say you admire them and their strength, perseverance, courage, and integrity.

What matters at the end: not what you have, but what you did for others.

The greatest gift to yourself is to sacrifice yourself for others.

Purgatory is seeing your life in the context of love, and the consequences of being loving or not being loving to God or one another. The worst pain is the realization of pain caused to others. Purgatory is a life review, when you experience the effects, from the perspective of others, of all that you have done and all that you have failed to do.

The only thing you really keep is what you give away.

Purpose

The meaning of life is Love God and Love One Another. We are here not only to spread love, but to experience love and be transformed and improved by love. We have a responsibility to become a better person, individually, and to help make the world better. (Better is more loving.)

The purpose of my life on this earth is to love, to know, to glorify, and to serve God. The purpose is not longevity. I will use whatever length of life I have to love.

The world is our canvas to glorify God with our earthly paintbrushes.

We are here to spread love, to make the world a more loving place, and to be transformed by love ourselves.

We are all like a piece of a hologram. We are unique and essential individuals yet part of the whole, and we have the whole within ourselves.

The whole backdrop of the earth is to be God's servant and apostle of His peace and to learn about God's love through the earth.

Be challenged by the call to Christianity. Don't be complacent. Don't say, "Well, I'm not doing anything really wrong, so I'm okay." Take risks beyond being just okay, and extend yourself to do loving things for others.

See the Hand of our Loving Creator in everything in life, and spread love to others in every way possible. Reach out with even more love and open your heart to those who may be against you or less than loving to you.

When life is looked at by the eyes of faith, everything makes perfect sense.

We can find our greatest strength from bringing God into our lives. This strength comes from knowing the ultimate truth – that God is love, God is always with us, and God is in control. God is not a so-called crutch; He is the meaning of the whole walk.

Happiness

My ultimate happiness is when I seek the happiness of others, and don't worry about my own.

Happiness comes from doing God's Will. What is God's Will, and how do I know that I'm doing it? I believe that wanting to do God's Will, and then trying to God's Will, are in essence doing God's Will.

What makes me happiest in life is when I feel I have brought people closer to God.

What brings true, lasting happiness? Having loving relationships (emotional closeness – not just the number of friends, but the depth of the friendships). Helping other people (knowing that your life had a purpose greater than yourself, and that you made the world a better place, a kinder place). Being a person of goodness (an honorable person, with integrity, character, and values).

Happiness is holiness. Holiness is doing God's Will. Unhappiness is sin. Sin is deviation from God, that which is loving.

Heaven is everyone together, forever, united in love.

Sanctity

A saint takes their earthly occupation and makes it a heavenly vocation.

A saint is someone who is a manifestation of God's love in this world.

Saints are people who do God's Will, and who enable other people to see God through them.

We should strive to be saints in society, to bring others to sanctification, and to be envoys of the love of Christ.

Saints radiate joy – irrepressible, ineffable joy – in all circumstances.

Whatever our occupation, we have one primary vocation: to love.

Sin is not only what you have done, but what you have failed to do.

The only thing I really fear in life is sin – separation from God. But I have faith that if I sin, and ask for forgiveness, and repent, that the Lord will forgive.

Life is sacred. All life has intrinsic and infinite value. Any kind of intentional killing is inherently wrong (e.g., abortion, euthanasia, death penalty). Life is created by God. We do not have the right to take life. All humans are equally valuable and sacred, and infinitely loved by God.

Walk each day on the path of the Lord, and try to do His will with each thought, word, and action. That is sanctity.

Suffering

You can be in utter pain, and be happier than you've ever been in your life. Suffering can bring one closer to God.

Suffering is not mutually exclusive with God. The fact that we suffer does not mean that God doesn't exist. Suffering offers ways that we can demonstrate and experience new dimensions of love.

Tragedy in life (e.g., illness, death, loss) is not necessarily a bad thing. "Good" and "bad" is that which is loving or not loving, respectively. A tragedy is that which deviates from love (i.e., sin). One can become a better person (more loving, patient, compassionate, understanding) through tragedies in life.

When you're weak, you're most strong. It's easy to be strong (in the eyes of the world) when you're feeling healthy and running around, but it's true strength of soul to be joyful and optimistic when you're feeling terrible.

Always make people feel loved, appreciated, and a complete joy to be with – whatever the circumstances (never any so-called burden). People generally don't choose adversity. It takes great inner strength to get through suffering and circumstances in life that were not chosen.

It's a great blessing to be able to take care of and help another person. Let them know how much you enjoy being with them, how admired and appreciated they are, and how they are just as beautiful and strong as always, even more so, because of their inner strength.

All humans have equal and infinite value and dignity. Never make someone feel like (in some way) a lesser human being. Always make people feel like a great gift in your life and in the world, because they are.

It doesn't matter whether someone is vertical or horizontal; that is the body, not who they are.

People who are sick or disabled (in the eyes of this world) can be the greatest gifts in the world.

You can be a profoundly productive person, even if you are lying sick in bed, if you have love in your heart.

Don't seek suffering. Seek to alleviate suffering. But if suffering comes your way, seek to bring the best out of it (love).

Suffering can bring about great good. Suffering unites us with Christ. What's the worst thing that happens: we die from the suffering – so what!

Work

All work should be God's work. It depends on motivation: whether you work with God and love in your heart.

If you're going to do something loving, do it with a feeling of joy in your heart, at the opportunity to do something nice for someone. Don't do it with resentment, or because doing it is easier than feeling guilty for not doing it.

Intentions are what matter. We can't dictate our functionality or the outcome. But we can have earnest and loving intentions.

Seek to be Christ in the workplace, to be the head, heart, and hands of Jesus.

Be loving to all. Think only good thoughts about people. Say only good things. Radiate kindness, goodness, and holiness.

Before doing anything, ask: Does it glorify God? It is true, kind, fair, and helpful? Does it make the world a better place? Does it spread faith, hope, charity, and love?

Being a nun and praying for others all day is just as (if not more) productive than being a nonstop corporate executive.

You are infinitely valuable for who you are, not just what you do.

Our vocation is to love God: to know Him, to come closer to Him, to learn about Him, to help others learn about Him, and to glorify Him.

We ultimately answer to God, not the world. God is our employer.

Surrender

God is in charge. I am not in charge. I may think or hope I am, but I am not.

See outcomes in life as the Hand of God, God gently leading you in another direction.

See everything as a gift from God – even things that the world sees as bad, look for the good.

The ultimate testimony to unconditional love is to love God just as much when bad things happen as when good things happen (bad and good defined in human terms).

How one can best serve God may evolve throughout one's life; there may be no one straight path.

Discernment and surrender to God's Will: knowing the difference between acceptance of one's situation (at least for the time being) and perseverance to change a situation.

Every day I wake up and ask, "God how can I do Your Will? Help me to do Your Will; to spread Your Joy and Your Love." And every evening I ask, "How did I do? What could I have done better? What should I focus on for tomorrow?" Overall: How can I bring Your joy, light, hope, and love to people? How can I make others happy, in both an immediate and an eternal sense?

I never question God, regardless of what life brings.

We may try to do the right thing, but it turns out wrong in the world's view, but still right and successful in God's view. Loving intentions are what matter.

You don't have to do everything or be everything to everybody: you need to say no to some things to say yes to others.

My will and God's Will should be aligned, regardless. God knows what is best for me, and for the world, so my will should be God's Will.

I'll do the legwork, but the outcome is in God's hands.

Integrity

Never ever say anything but the entire truth. This is your integrity. You can still be polite. No difference between a small lie and a big lie; they are both untrue.

People say that integrity is how you act when no one is looking. But God is always looking. And everyone will know everything anyway (because we are all interconnected).

Be a person of integrity; radiate the fruits of the spirit: love, joy, peace, patience, kindness, goodness, faithfulness, gentleness, and self-control.

Be courageous. Stand up for other people.

Do the right thing, by God, and let the chips fall where they may.

Don't do anything you'd be ashamed of; you have to live with yourself, your soul knows, even if no one else does. Be true to yourself and to higher values.

Be just as eager (if not more so) to return to a store to give them back money if they undercharge you (than if the other way around).

Moral strength and character is do the right thing, regardless of personal consequences or suffering.

Faith

Faith is a steadfast, optimistic belief (actually transcends belief, it's a knowledge beyond this brain) in the goodness of God, an omnipresent, benevolent, loving God, and the hope for what has begun but has not yet been fully realized. It is what guides us through the waves of life.

Faith in the everlasting makes what we do here even more so infinitely important. We are here, sowing the seeds of love that sprout in eternity.

Faith is beyond human reason; it is the truth, it's what our soul knows. Because human reason involves molecular functions, which can be faulty, then human reason is not necessarily the ultimate truth. God is the ultimate truth.

Faith and prayer may or may not change an earthly outcome, but it changes the journey, and the way you view the outcome. It deepens the loving relationship with God along the journey.

A belief in God is the most intellectual, rational, natural thing one can do. It is meta-science, meta-logic. Plus, if science is the search of truth, then religion is completely consistent with that, because God is the universal and unwavering truth.

When life has been hard, I never blamed God, lost faith in God, or gave up on God. I have loved God just as fervently in bad (human) times as in good.

I've been given the gift of life. Now it's about what I can give of my life for others.

Faith is the opposite of worry. If you have faith (in the goodness and love of God), why worry?

Unity

Love is monotonically increasing with time. It doesn't matter whether the beloved is still on this earth or in heaven. We can love our loved ones more and more each day.

Love can grow in a relationship with someone even after death. By analogy, Jesus was human, he's now with the Father, and we have a growing loving relationship with Him.

Marriage until death do us part – I believe that death doesn't separate two loved ones, and that marriage can continue and blossom even more after death.

Happiness is being with a beloved. Everything is a positive, no such thing as ups and downs. Everything is an up if you're together. It's like sailing together – you're in the boat together, and the storms just bring you closer together and make you better sailors.

Any time spent loving someone is never lost time.

Encouragement

Be heroic in the little things. The small things are the big things.

Commit yourself to excellence. Do the best that you can do with the gifts that God has given you.

Better to do a few things really well, than a whole lot of things not so well.

Take the long view; look ahead, see what will matter in the future.

Stay optimistic and tenacious, keep positive and hopeful.

Don't get discouraged (that's a favorite tool of the devil).

Don't make comparisons (that's another favorite tool of the devil).

You are unique. You have special gifts. Run your own race; keep your blinders on.

You have infinite spiritual gifts. Whereas economists say that people have unlimited wants for material goods, and that resources for producing those goods are finite, I say that people have limited wants for material goods, but unlimited wants for spiritual goods, and unlimited abilities to produce those spiritual goods (e.g., love), so that those resources are infinite.

The call in life is to do the best with what you have. (Best is God's Will.)

For encouragement: call on Jesus, ask for His help, trust Him, take one step at a time, one day (or one moment) at a time, have faith, things will and do get better.

Whatever the question, love is the answer.

Whatever the problem, love is the solution.

Flying on the Wings
of the Angels of Love

A Collection of Sayings
by Anne Steinemann

Compiled and edited by John R. Barrie

Table of Contents

Foreword

Many fortunate readers are now treated to a second small collection of sublime, inspirational sayings from the heart and soul of Anne Steinemann, Ph.D. Anne's remarkable skill has been to focus her entire life on two essential teachings of Jesus: Love God, and Love One Another. So simple, yet so utterly profound. "The most important thing we do is to love," is Anne's wise counsel to us all.

And so, these uncompromisingly beautiful aphorisms originate from the single uplifting motif of divine love: Where to find it? (Everywhere!) Who to share it with? (Everyone!) When to express it? (Always!)

Anne Steinemann's extraordinary God-given gift has been to tap into the living waters of Jesus and distill the very essence of religion and spirituality, then convincingly present to us, by way of her many stirring sayings, that there is only one thing which matters on this earth: love.

John R. Barrie

Preface

Over the years, I wrote down spiritual insights and reflections, and from these was born the book, "Love is Like the Universe." This present book is the second child, with longer and more diverse sayings. I entrusted John R. Barrie with the full collection, and he devoted himself to going through hundreds of verses and picking his favorites. So he is to thank and credit for this book, and it is dedicated to him.

Anne Steinemann
Easter 2022

One Vocation

The purpose of life is not humanly perfection but loving perfection.

God is a loving presence. God wants to spread love. We want to spread love.

See all things as a gift from a loving Father.

Remember, you will have many occupations in life, but one vocation: to be loving.

Exemplify the fruits of the spirit – do the extraordinary in the ordinary situations of life.

Use your positions in this world to bring the love of Christ, and to bring people to the love of Christ, beyond this world.

Use your influence according to the world's standards to bring compassion and justice and understanding and dignity and resources to the people who the world has outcast.

Be kind to everyone. Everyone!

Reach out to the "poor" (according to earthly criteria, but wealthy by God's criteria) and the "outcasts" in society – the homeless, the prisoners, the disabled, the financially impoverished, the poor in spirit.

Be open to His voice and be willing to give all to follow Him.

The greatest joy and gift in life is to help another person – and that people who are sick or disabled can be the greatest blessings in the world – and we need to let them know how valued and appreciated and heroic they are, for going through each day with limitations and challenges.

Treasure the Journey

Human happiness is the happiness and holiness of the soul: it is knowing God and spreading love in the world.

God is omnipresent, and the workings of God on this earth are seen in humans.

The world is for me to be drawn closer to Him.

Treasure the journey of life. Learn from it. Take one step at a time. Leave the rest to God.

We are these infinitely loving people, stuck in these finite bodies. And our soul wants to do everything and anything for our loved ones, and not be limited by the constraints of time and space. But the nature of this earth means we can only do a finite amount. Now I say "do" in a human sense, not a Godly sense, because the most important thing we do is to love, and the human body with its physicality is but one manifestation, to display our soul's love.

My ultimate vocation is to love God: to know Him, to come closer to Him, to learn about Him, to help others learn about Him, and to glorify Him.

We live in order to love, not the other way around.

What is "good" for individuals is the ability to love God and love one another.

What matters is how much we love others, not how much others love us back. Otherwise, love is transactional and conditional.

Know, Love, and Serve

We are the head, heart, and hands of Jesus.

I say each day in prayers: "Dear Lord. I love you. Thank you for this life. Here is the day ahead. What do You want me to do? How can I glorify you? Please help me to do Your Will. Please help me to know, love, and serve You."

While I believe that love involves gleeful self-giving, even at the sake of one's body and health, I respect that we need to take care of this vehicle that God has given us in order to help other people.

The concept of "self" is just a vehicle for God – and that I do nothing for myself or of myself, but it's God working through me. All of existence (or what I know of existence as a human) is just a vortex that gets funneled to self (a soul) as the center, and that center radiates out to the rest. Everything is interconnected; even people over in Africa who I may never physically see are still nonetheless all connected to me.

We are connected to everything, we are individuals yet part of the whole, and we have the whole within ourselves. Similarly, a cell has all the information for the entire body, and it is part of the whole – just like the Body of Christ.

God is the Meaning

God is the meaning, and God is ultimately in charge.

God is ultimate love. It's good that the person in charge is all about love!

I am not truly fulfilled without God.

I'm surprised when people profess that they believe there is no God, no supernatural component to life (e.g., "what we see is all there is"), or that it is somehow "unscientific" or "irrational" to believe in anything other than naturalism or nothing. I have no doubt that their lives are happy and fulfilling (at some level) and loving as is. But my hope is that they could be able to bring God into their lives and see how life is transformed (by analogy – like a black-and-white movie becoming color), and how the earth and this human existence are even more (not less) meaningful in the context of God.

God made me. He knows what he's doing. I am here to serve Him. Luckily, God is about love.

I always knew that everything was from a loving Father, and it was for my good and the good of the world.

Jesus loves us, even though the rest of the world may not.

I am here to spread all the love I can, and to learn about love and God.

Higher Purpose

I have done the right thing by the world and been a "success" in terms of the things of the world. But perhaps that's why makes me an effective instrument of God. Because I have made it in this world – and then can tell others that those criteria and accomplishments are meaningless in the eyes of God.

You are valuable and loved for who you are, not what you do or what you accomplish.

Do not let temporary and earthly circumstances influence your higher purpose.

Anyone can be happy when they're feeling well. It takes the ultimate strength, and is the ultimate test of character and Christian faith, to be happy, etc. when you're not feeling well.

Remember, people don't choose to be unwell; they don't like it; and they probably also don't like losing their autonomy and freedom to be able to take care of themselves.

Always Be Joyful

We can't get caught up into viewing things in the eyes of this world.

Have hope. Hold onto Jesus. What matters is staying in the game when things seem dark, and you will get to the light. All will be well. You'll be on the upswing soon.

Always be joyful – reflects faith in a loving God.

No such thing as unpleasantness or work – it's all joy, with love.

Don't let fear and discouragement get to you. That's what the devil wants.

The devil comes in the most clever of disguises to get you all excited and to prey on your vulnerabilities and to assuage your fears, but then the switcheroo. Just take each day and walk with the Lord and trust Him.

It's always a fine line between: (a) acceptance of one's situation, and realizing it's God's Will that He wants you to be there, and making the most of it, and to glorify Him; and (b) being fed up with one's situation, and being impelled to make a change – enough already!

Be an Instrument

When a door is closed, when do you keep knocking? And when do you stop hurting your hand and look for another door (or a window)? Maybe it's a little of both, saying, "Lord, I know I am here for a reason. I really don't like this and that, but please help me to see Your love, and spread Your love in this place – and lead me out of here, as soon as You will let me leave."

It's great to persevere with optimism. But don't beat your head against a locked door. Know when it's time to walk away and look for the open door (or the key).

Be an instrument of peace in the workplace.

Manifest Jesus in the workplace in small ways (but the small ways can really be the big ways).

Live your life as if you are in a fishbowl. Whatever you do, be proud of it, as if the whole world is looking and knows about it. (They will, in the end.)

Be known for excellence in whatever you do. (Excellence is of God.)

Seeking God's Will

Everything makes sense when put in the context of faith.

Nature is God's way of calling you to wonder, to be in awe of the beauty, to be drawn into thoughts of the infinite beauty.

Wherever you are, that's where you're supposed to be (if you are seeking God's will) and that maybe the infinite past and infinite future have converged in order to make this imperfect person at this perfect time and place.

Never worry. Just ride things out. It doesn't matter how things come about. Have faith the right thing will occur.

Do not make any decision out of fear or anxiety. Have faith in the process. But don't put your faith in any outcome other than what God chooses for you. Make the decision that brings you peace.

Listen to your gut. Don't let your head's brain override what your soul's brain (your gut) is telling you.

Radiate the G's: Gratitude, Generosity, Gleefulness, Graciousness, Goodness – and Godliness.

Take the long view. Tenacity counts for everything. Stay in the race. And run your own race. Don't make comparisons. Keep your blinkers on – like a thoroughbred race horse.

Don't let other people discourage you.

Peer pressure: Don't be afraid to say "no, thank you" because you're really saying "yes" to something more important – yourself, your values, and your life.

The Precious Pearl

My overarching and wholehearted desire (the most important thing with my life) is to do God's Will.

I loved unconditionally and completely. I never questioned God, regardless of what life brought.

What is the precious pearl for which I would sell all? It is love.

About the Author

Along with being a lifelong Catholic, Anne Carol Steinemann has been a Professor of Civil and Environmental Engineering across the U.S. and Australia for nearly three decades. Through her remarkable body of professional work and her extensive spiritual work, she has touched and continues to touch hundreds of thousands of lives.

Born on September 29, 1961 (the Feast Day of St. Michael the Archangel), in San Diego, California, Anne has been drawn to a life of holiness her entire life. As a young girl, she gleefully visited religious communities and churches, studied the lives of the saints, and pursued truths about God, the universe, and the purpose of human existence. She knew early on that her purpose was to love God and to love others, universally and unconditionally. She also knew that she needed to make the most of her life to serve others and give gratitude to God. Above all, she sought to do God's will.

And so, armed with her vision of life, Anne quickly ascended the academic ladder at the finest educational institutions. After receiving her Ph.D. in Civil and Environmental Engineering from Stanford University in 1993, Anne has held prestigious academic positions at universities both in the United States and in Australia. Among her many stellar achievements and accolades, Anne has been acclaimed as the most highly cited academic researcher globally in her research field. She has also been ranked in the top 2% of scientists and engineers, worldwide. She became an internationally recognized expert on pollutant exposures and associated health effects, addressing topics of indoor air quality, consumer product emissions, and healthy housing and communities.

But Anne has been no theoretical scientist. Her groundbreaking research resulted in change. Her work has brought about new legislation, policies, and practices—at more than one hundred agencies, industries, and institutions around the world. Her research also received international media attention in the top newspapers, magazines, and broadcast networks across six continents, with a global reach of several hundred million people. She has published more than one hundred articles in leading journals in the areas of engineering, science, policy, and public health, and she has authored several books, including a pivotal text on microeconomics for public decisions.

As the principal academic torchbearer worldwide on the issue of fragranced product exposures, Anne has been the go-to scientist for high-level decision-makers and a household name to her devoted followers. She has received more than 4,000 emails from people around the world, thanking her for her research. One person called

Anne the "greatest living hero." Another wrote that Anne's work should win her a Nobel Prize. Anne's research and teaching has always emphasized public service, underscored by a strong social mission. Moreover, Anne has always felt that her ultimate vocation, within any occupation, is to bring the love of God to other people.

Alongside her academic profession, Anne has created, led, and volunteered with ministries for the homeless, prisoners, student crisis counseling, defense of life, the disabled, refugees, faith and reason, and religious education. For instance, for more than twenty years, she visited prisons and jails to talk with inmates, and she has an active ministry on death row. Prisoners attest to Anne's ability to bring the love of God into their lives. As one said, "I wish you could see how Anne has touched these men and warmed their hearts, even the hardest men. The guys call Anne the 'Angel of Death Row.'" She also ministers to refugees in Africa, providing them food, clothing, mats, and Holy Bibles. Anne extends her loving and open arms, emulating Our Lady of Grace, to spiritually embrace and befriend everyone, especially the neglected, underappreciated, and suffering in society. She sees no barriers: to her everyone is equally precious and infinitely beloved.

Anne is a devoted and enthusiastic Catholic, and she has served as a lector, sacristan, and extraordinary minister of Holy Communion at her local parishes. She treasures daily Mass, weekly Confession, Eucharistic Adoration, saying the Rosary, and prayer. She especially enjoys talking with young people about the joys and truth of the faith, and why a belief in God is scientific and the source of our ultimate happiness.

Over the decades, Anne wrote down many of her spiritual insights and reflections. She published a selection of them in two booklets, *Love is Like the Universe* (Christmas 2021) and *Flying on the Wings of the Angels of Love* (Easter 2022). Both are included in this special edition. Anne's books of inspirational maxims are treasure troves of timeless spiritual truths. These sayings are not only encouraging; they are transformational. They provoke awe, gratitude, devotion, and hope. They speak directly to one's soul. Beyond this, no one could write these inspired words without living them.

A ceaseless ambassador of goodwill, optimism, and compassion, Anne serves as a minister of God's love, whether working globally or one-on-one. She is known far and wide as a truly good and caring person, utterly selfless, and always focused on others. She is unfailingly cheerful and gracious, which belies her great physical suffering due to a rare medical condition, yet this provides even greater witness to her faith. Whether engaging in her many silent philanthropical activities, or giving of herself on the frontlines of life, Anne Steinemann is happiest when she is helping others. She puts into practice the very essence of Jesus' message: Love God and Love One Another.

–John R. Barrie

Citations of quoted material are used with the kind permission of Anne Steinemann.

www.ingramcontent.com/pod-product-compliance
Lightning Source LLC
Chambersburg PA
CBHW060350130626
46553CB00003B/1165

2)

BIN TRAVELER FORM

Cut By: Tiffany Jones   Qty 30   Date 7/1

Scanned By: Ivan T.   Qty _____ Date 07-02-26

Scanned Batch ID's

285490873

Notes / Exceptions